COVID-19
PRAYER JOURNAL

"We don't just believe in prayer,
we believe in answered prayers"

Revd Dr Jim Master

COVID-19 PRAYER JOURNAL

COVID-19 PRAYER JOURNAL
"We don't just believe in prayer, we believe in answered prayers"
By Revd Dr Jim Master
Copyright © 2020 Jim Master
The right of Jim Master to be identified as the author of this work has been asserted by him in accordance with the Copyright, Designs and Patents Act 1988.
All rights reserved. No part of this publication may be reproduced, stored in a retrieval system, or transmitted in any other form or by any means, electronic, mechanical, photocopying, recording or otherwise, without the prior permission of the publisher.
Published for Revd Dr Jim Master by
Verité CM Limited, 124 Sea Place, Worthing, West Sussex BN12 4BG
+44 (0) 1903 241975
email: enquiries@veritecm.com
Web: www.veritecm.com
British Library Cataloguing in Publication Data
A catalogue record for this book is available from the British Library
ISBN: 978-1-910719-90-9

Scripture quotations marked "ESV" are taken from The Holy Bible, English Standard Version® copyright © 2001 by Crossway Bibles, a publishing ministry of Good News Publishers. ESV Text Edition: 2016. The ESV® text has been reproduced in cooperation with and by permission of Good News Publishers. All rights reserved.

Scripture quotations marked "KJV" are taken from The Authorised (King James) Version. Rights in the Authorized Version in the United Kingdom are vested in the Crown. Reproduced by permission of the Crown's patentee, Cambridge University Press.

Scripture quotations marked "NASB" are taken from the NEW AMERICAN STANDARD BIBLE®, Copyright © 1960,1962,1963,1968,1971,1972,1973,1975,1977,1995 by The Lockman Foundation. Used by permission.

Scripture quotations marked "NIV" are taken from the Holy Bible, New International Version Anglicised. Copyright © 1979, 1984, 2011 by Biblica, formerly International Bible Society. Used by permission of Hodder & Stoughton Publishers, an Hachette UK company. All rights reserved.

Scripture quotations marked "NKJV" are taken from the New King James Version®. Copyright © 1982 by Thomas Nelson. Used by permission. All rights reserved.

Print Management by Verité CM Ltd
www.veritecm.com
Printed in England

INTRODUCTION

This book of prayers was written and compiled during the "lockdown" announced by the government in March 2020 in order to protect us from the Covid-19 pandemic. Using quotes, scripture and thoughts, I wanted to bring some comfort, as often as I could, to members of my church so they could join me in prayers and devotions and hope to bring comfort to them during one of the worst events this country has faced during peace time. As devastating as this season is, we must always look to God and appreciate life is a gift!

17th March 2020

God's Word

I believe the Word of God which says, "As for God, His way is perfect; the word of the Lord is proven; He is a shield to all who trust in Him" (Psalm 18:30).

Prayer . . .

Father, thank You for giving me Your eternal, unshakable Word to study and be rooted in. I ask You to open my eyes to Your many powerful promises and to keep my eyes on Your unfailing grace and faithfulness. I believe that as I continue to believe Your promises, I will walk more and more in Your total protection. Amen.

21st March 2020

Getting your strength!

As a senior leader, it has saddened me to close down activities in the church, as Jesus wants His Church to be "built". I know that most of my peers have emotionally struggled with this too.

Like most Christian leaders, we need to draw our strength from God's number-one resource: spending time in prayer and seeking God's Word. So I would like to encourage you with this quote I came across this morning.

Woodrow Wilson, the twenty-sixth president of the United States, once said, "I am sorry for men who do not read the Bible every day. I wonder why they deprive themselves of the strength and of the pleasure. It is one of the most singular books in the world, for every time you open it, some old text that you have read a score of times suddenly beams with new meaning. There is no other book that I know of which this is true. There is no other book that yields its meaning so personally. And it seems to fit so intimately to the very spirit that is seeking its guidance."

As I prayed . . .

As you encounter troubles, expect that your God will give you answers, He will provide shelter in times of failure, and He will supply strength in times of fellowship. Because you know that you have standing before God, you can come to Him any time in the name of Jesus. Paul reminds us, "He who did not spare His own Son, but delivered Him up for us all, how shall He not with Him also freely give us all things?" (Romans 8:32 NKJV). Jesus was the best that God could give; He will continue to freely give His people good things. You can be assured – convicted – that as you have right standing with God, you can have an audience with Him, and He will hear you and answer your prayers.

24th March 2020

Pray for the reversal of Covid-19

"He who dwells in the secret place . . ." (Psalm 91)

History repeating itself in a good way! In 1905, 240 major department stores signed an agreement to close between 10:00am and 2:00pm every day for prayers until revival fell in Portland, Oregon, USA. Imagine an entire city, in the middle of the busiest period each day, closing down, as businessmen, customers, employers and employees, all attended prayer meetings for days on end.

As a result, there was a great awakening throughout the entire Pacific Northwest.

George Mueller at a point resolved that instead of praying once a day with his wife, as they had been doing for years, they would meet three times each day for prayers. They even engaged their entire staff in the prayer commitment.

Missionary John Hyde, also known as "Praying Hyde", covenanted to sleep one hour each night, awake for two hours of prayer, sleep one hour, pray another two hours. This was his formula each night. He was known by the native Indians as "the man that doesn't sleep". Pentecost took place again as a result.

I was reading a book about Martin Luther, how he entered a two-hour covenant and by so doing was used to usher in a great awakening worldwide. As I was reading, a voice from inside me said, "You can do that." So I went down on my knees and entered into that covenant of prayers. I attended a prayer conference some years later, the challenge was so great that I decided to upgrade to 3 hours' prayer daily.

A spokeswoman said yesterday that many nurses are wanting time to pray!

Prayer . . .

Father, we pray that this pandemic is reversed and turns into a revival. May Your Holy Spirit spread throughout the land. All praise and glory unto You. Amen.

25th March 2020

The NHS needs our prayers

It's obvious that the height of our prayers should be directed towards the medical staff working for the NHS. When the reality of working in a high-risk environment hits home and we become so busy, we can so easily forget about the protection of God.

This was brought to my attention reading from the book of Daniel about the three men who would not bow before an idol, under the King Nebuchadnezzar. They were thrown into the fire and even when the men around them got burnt, Shadrach, Meshach and Abednego walked through without being harmed at all. In the season of "fire" there was angel of protection.

Our prayer is for the believers who are in contact with people every day in the medical profession that they feel the angel of protection surrounding them during this fiery season.

> *"Give relief to you who are troubled, and to us as well. This will happen when the Lord Jesus is revealed from heaven in blazing fire with his powerful angels."* (2 Thessalonians 1:7 NIV)

> *"Clap your hands, all you nations; shout to God with cries of joy. For the Lord Most High is awesome, the great King over all the earth. He subdued nations under us, peoples under our feet."* (Psalm 47:1-3 NIV)

It was so good to hear at 8.00 pm, people of this nation clap their hands to those standing on the front line of the NHS. We applaud

COVID-19 PRAYER JOURNAL

their skills and abilities that God has given each one of them and continue to pray for them all as the intensity of the coronavirus increases.

The "clapping of hands" draws attention to something, usually as an outward expression of inward joy.

Let us pray and clap our hands to the 500,000 volunteers in this country who have stepped up to assist people.

Let us pray and clap our hands for the UK government for supplying people's needs and benefits that so many other countries are struggling with.

Let us pray and clap our hands for the police and armed forces for wisdom and protection.

Let us pray and clap our hands for chaplains meeting the spiritual needs of those in the police and armed forces, prisons, hospitals, etc.

We applaud you all for the service you are giving.

"For ye shall go out with joy, and be led forth with peace: the mountains and the hills shall break forth before you into singing, and all the trees of the field shall clap their hands." (Isaiah 55:12 KJV)

Prayer . . .

Lord, throughout Scripture, You protected Your people with miracles, signs and wonders. We pray for the coming few weeks, that when the fire becomes more intense, the medical staff will be totally protected and Your power will be shown and glorified. Amen.

30th March 2020

Facing predicaments

A cook for example, might describe herself as being in a pickle. Some people may describe themselves as being between a rock and a hard place. Whatever the expression the meaning is the same. Someone facing trouble that cannot be easily escaped from. Some predicaments are uncomfortable and nerve-wracking and often threaten to drive us into despair.

In Exodus 14, where Moses was between the devil and the Red Sea, he led the Israelites into the desert. During this season Moses took the reins to lead the people from the enemy.

The first response was to cry out to the Lord to rescue them. But the people blamed Moses for getting them into this fix as tribes of armies were bearing down on them.

Moses stood tall and called on the name of the Lord instead of defending himself against the people's accusations. Moses confidently then directed their attention to being delivered by God.

So, the waters were divided. They watched all night as God sent powerful wind to dry up the muddy riverbed. It must have been difficult for the people to choose between watching a pillar of fire, holding off the Egyptians and watching the wind blow a dry path through the sea. There was, however, no difficult choice about what to do when the morning came: "The children of Israel went into the midst of the sea on the dry ground, and the waters were a wall to them on their right hand and on their left" (Exodus 14:22 NKJV). What we have here is a great deliverer. And we must trust in God in everything He does through our prayers because He will deliver us through the season of hardship. We are about to face a predicament. But we also have the mantle of God in our hands.

God once again worked through His servant Moses to miraculously deliver His people. What an amazing sight that must have been!

Covid-19 is a predicament that we are facing in the next few weeks that is potentially reaching higher intensity.

When Pharaoh's army bears down on us, we often fear the worst and rush right into the fight. But God wants us to do the exact opposite. He wants us to show confidence in Him as we wait and watch Him at work as He delivers us.

Standby. Keep silent. These are responses that demonstrate our trust in God.

Prayer . . .

Dear Lord, we are facing a "predicament" and we need Your help. Only You can deliver us from this crisis and help us through this hardship. Help us to call on You to stand in the gap. Amen.

31st March 2020

Let my people go!

As I was reading Exodus 12 I thought about God giving Moses instructions to leave Egypt just before the tenth plague. There was no power in the dried blood of a slain lamb. Yet God, in His unfathomable wisdom, designed a plan that required only one thing – obedience. He never asked them to think it through. He never asked them to dialogue about it. He never asked them to consider the idea and decide if they agreed. He simply told them what to do and when to do it. And then He told them what would happen as a result of their strict obedience to His commands.

> *"For I will pass through the land of Egypt on that night, and will strike down all the firstborn in the land of Egypt, both man and beast; and against all the gods of Egypt I will execute judgment – I am the Lord. The blood shall be a sign for you on the houses where you are; and when I see the blood, I will pass over you."* (vv. 12–13 NKJV)

Sound familiar? If you're like me, you'll remember singing that old hymn, "When I see the blood, I will pass, I will pass over you." God told them, "I'm going to visit Egypt. Tonight. I will invade every dwelling where there is no blood on the door. But there will be blood on the doorways of my people, and they will be spared. That's my plan."

During the time of Moses, when the blood of the Lamb was used to protect all believers, which was the sign of things to come. The "angel of death" can only pass over, yes pass over! So now we can pray for this Covid-19 to pass over and soon we will have a memorial day, a celebration of how the Lord protected many of us .

"This day will be a memorial to you, and you shall celebrate it as a feast to the Lord; throughout your generations you are to celebrate it as a permanent ordinance." (v.14 NASB)

Prayer . . .

Thank You, Lord, that You died and shared Your blood on the cross, so that we would be protected. We ask You to forgive us for allowing "fear" to take over and to help us have more confidence in Your protection over our lives. In Jesus' name. Amen.

1st April 2020

Needing to ask God for forgiveness during this season of Covid-19

Passover brought obedience! Exodus chapter 12 – 13

During this time of hearing about the deaths from coronavirus, the Lord brought it to my attention that my obedience needs to be stronger. That this isn't a "feeling" thing at all. There have been times when I haven't felt like preaching. There have been days when I haven't felt like walking into our Bible school. There have been times when I haven't felt like being true to my friends. There have been times when I haven't felt like responding to a brother or sister in need, even when I have the resources to help.

But, you know what? It never really mattered how I felt. My feelings will change day to day, maybe hour to hour, like the English weather! However, I still get on and do the job, regardless of how I feel.

My priority is to obey God's revealed will, it's that plain and simple. The Israelites may not have felt like smearing lamb's blood on the lintel and doorposts of their home that dark night of the first Passover. They surely didn't understand the Lord's reasoning. They had no idea that it would point towards a future Messiah who would pay the debt of sin with His own blood and die for the sins of the world. They just did it; they obeyed because they had believed the Word of the Lord. They followed the instructions without understanding all the whys and wherefores. A few hours later, they were very glad that they did. Obedience always pays off, and they were free from bondage.

Praying for forgiveness . . .

Dear Lord, forgive us as we sometimes trust our feelings more than You. This world has been brought to a standstill and now is the time for us to get on our knees and repent and ask for forgiveness. We thank You that we just need to trust and obey, no matter how odd the situation may be. Help us to stand in the gap for unbelievers and let revival come to this world. Amen.

2nd April 2020

A new resurrection for believers in the next 2 months

Let's pray for what the resurrection will do during Easter.

The resurrection of the Lord Jesus Christ is the provision that guarantees we will not be sent to eternal damnation, but to a wonderful eternal life. The resurrection of Jesus Christ in bodily form, from the grave, is a pledge and a promise to all who believe in Him that we too will be raised in bodily form to enter into the eternal bliss and the joy of heaven in the presence of God everlastingly, serving, worshipping and being completely satisfied.

The resurrection is of such significance it dominates the New Testament, and particularly dominates the preaching of the gospel that begins early in the book of Acts and runs all the way through the New Testament. The resurrection is not just a feature of Christianity, it is the essential truth. The whole point of the gospel is to rescue people from hell so that they can go to heaven. The whole point of the gospel is to be delivered from judgement into eternal blessing.

The resurrection, then, is not the epilogue, it's not some kind of postscript on the end of our Lord's life. It is the goal of His life, the high point of the gospel. The resurrection is the divine interpretation of the death of Christ; Easter interprets Good Friday. The resurrection is the divine vindication of the sacrifice Jesus made on the cross, the benefits of that sacrifice begin to be gathered at the resurrection, Christ being the first fruits. The resurrection guarantees our resurrection!

Prayer . . .

Father, we thank You that You are the resurrection and the life. As we prepare to celebrate Easter next week, we pray for a resurrected life and that many during this period will come to Christ. We know Christ is this reason for the season and so we pray many will know Christ as their personal Saviour. Amen!

3rd April 2020

A new resurrection for those who believe

Let's pray for what the resurrection will do during Easter.

> *"Praise be to the God and Father of our Lord Jesus Christ! In his great mercy he has given us new birth into a living hope through the resurrection of Jesus Christ from the dead."* (1 Peter 1:3 NIV)

The resurrection of the Lord Jesus Christ is the provision that guarantees we will not be sent to eternal damnation, but to a wonderful eternal life. The resurrection of Jesus Christ in bodily form, from the grave, is a pledge and a promise to all who believe in Him that we too will be raised in bodily form to enter into the eternal bliss and the joy of heaven in the presence of God everlastingly, serving, worshipping and being completely satisfied.

The resurrection is of such significance it dominates the New Testament, and particularly dominates the preaching of the gospel that begins early in the book of Acts and runs all the way through the New Testament. The resurrection is not just a feature of Christianity, it is the essential truth. The whole point of the gospel is to rescue people from hell so that they can go to heaven. The whole point of the gospel is to be delivered from judgement into eternal blessing.

The resurrection, then, is not the epilogue, it's not some kind of postscript on the end of our Lord's life. It is the goal of His life, the high point of the gospel. The resurrection is the divine interpretation of the death of Christ; Easter interprets Good Friday. The resurrection is the divine vindication of the sacrifice Jesus made on the cross, the benefits of that sacrifice begin to be gathered at the resurrection, Christ being the first fruits. The resurrection guarantees our resurrection!

Prayer . . .

Father, we thank you that you are the resurrection and the life. As we prepare to celebrate Easter, next week, we pray for a resurrected life and that many, during this period will come to Christ. We know Christ in this reason for the season and so we pray many will know Christ as their personal Saviour. Amen!

4th April 2020

I remember hearing this psalm being read out on the radio more than 20 years ago, and this morning my spirit reminded me that we have special bodyguards!

> *"For he will command his angels concerning you to guard you in all your ways; they will lift you up in their hands, so that you will not strike your foot against a stone. You will tread on the lion and the cobra; you will trample the great lion and the serpent."* (Psalm 91:11-13 NIV)

God has promised to send angelic assistance when we face attacks.

In verses 11-13, the psalmist describes three specific activities of the angels on our behalf.

- Firstly, angels are given "charge" of us (v.11). The term "charge" is from the Hebrew "tzawa", which means "to appoint, install, give command of". Other passages of scripture suggest that the Lord has actually appointed angels – heavenly guardians – to give us aid when attacked by strange forces (Matthew 18:10; Acts 12:15).

- Secondly, angels "guard" us in all our ways (v.11). The Hebrew word "shamar" means "to keep, watch over, observe, preserve, take care of". Angels are overseers of God's people. Like silent sentries, they stand guard over those who seek refuge in the Lord, preserving our steps.

- Thirdly, angels "bear you up" in their hands (v.12). The verb "nasah" actually means "to lift, to carry, take up". When used figuratively in reference to a person, it means "to support, sustain". In the context of Psalm 91, the angels see to your mental, emotional and spiritual needs so that you will not be overwhelmed by the deception and the fear of Covid-19.

Prayer . . .

Dear Father, I thank You that we are not alone and that there is an army of angelic hosts to protect us during this intense time. We pray for the NHS, carers, all our public services, the armed forces and especially the homeless and isolated elderly. Send Your angels to keep their spirits lifted so they know they are not alone. Send Your bodyguards before us and take away any fear that might oppress us. In Jesus' name! Amen.

5th April 2020

History has proven calling the nations to pray and fast for the war to be over.

World War One: the opening phase of the Allied offensive in spring of 1918, news came back home to Britain that the German army had broken through Allied lines on mainland Europe causing heavy casualties. Their reserves were almost exhausted, so that the Allies were on the verge of defeat. When the situation became desperate, King George V called Britain to a day of prayer with fasting on 4th August. At Westminster, he led the people in turning to God, just like the godly kings of the Old Testament did. Four days later, on 8th August, the famous Battle of Amiens began; the first of a series of brilliant victories in the British sector. Later, at Bethune near the Belgian border, the German troops were given the order to advance in a massive attack on the Allies. Suddenly, up through the smoke of the battle, a brigade of white-uniformed cavalry soldiers appeared, all mounted on white horses, riding forward in precise formation. The German forces concentrated explosive shells and machine-gun fire upon them, but they came on steadily, not one falling, led by their awe-inspiring leader with shining, golden hair. He was seated on a white charger. In spite of heavy firing, the white cavalry advanced remorselessly as fate towards the German army. Suddenly, awful fear and panic seized the entire army, who turned and fled terror stricken, throwing down their weapons.

As the angels of God came down to fight in response to the national day of prayer and fasting, it was also the time of turning the tide of war in favour of the Allies' advance. By 11th November 1918, a truce was signed and the war was over!

> *"So he said to me, 'This is the word of the Lord to Zerubbabel: "Not by might nor by power, but by my Spirit," says the Lord Almighty.'"* (Zechariah 4:6 NIV)

Prayer . . .

Dear Lord, it is not by "might, nor by power, but by His Spirit" that this war will be over. We thank You that You know all things and everything is under Your feet and is in Your hands. We pray that Christian politicians will rise up and call for a day of prayer and fasting! We thank You for Your mercy and love. Amen.

6th April 2020

One of the greatest Bible stories I love to read over and over is about Obededom.

> *"And the ark of the Lord continued in the house of Obededom the Gittite three months: and the Lord blessed Obededom, and all his household. And it was told king David, saying, The Lord hath blessed the house of Obededom, and all that pertaineth unto him, because of the ark of God. So David went and brought up the ark of God from the house of Obededom into the city of David with gladness."* (2 Samuel 6:11-12 KJV)

In this season of isolation, many of us now have more time to seek His presence and hear His voice. As believers we should use this to our advantage and ask Jesus to fill our homes with His presence. Those of you on the frontline may take this time to pray for His presence to enter your workplace.

The government keeps mentioning 3 months of isolation! Meanwhile, when we read the story of the ark of the covenant representing God's presence, which was put as a temporary measure in Odededom's house during that time, God blessed him and his household. We, too, can anticipate extraordinary things happening, if we seek His face.

> *"And the ark of the Lord continued in the house of Obededom the Gittite three months and the Lord blessed Obededom, and his household. And it was told King David."*

The ark of God represents the presence of God. Three months of staying under and around God's presence continually was enough to transform the entire household of Obededom. So great was this transformation that the news of it reached King David, who decided he needed what Obededom had, so ordered the ark to his corner!

Prayer . . .

Dear Father, we pray in this Holy Week that we will seek Your presence to enter into our homes and workplaces. We pray for an atmosphere of godliness to birth extraordinary things beyond what we can possibly imagine. Grant us Your grace in this season of desperation. Amen.

7th April 2020

I have no doubt that all believers in the country started to pray for our prime minister last night as this virus, which is no respecter of persons, continues to cause great harm and disruption and continues to surprise us each day as it intensifies. So, throughout this Holy Week, join me in praying that this will "pass over".

As we read in Exodus 12:13, during the first Passover they killed the lamb and put the blood on the doorposts. This caused the destroyer to pass over their families because God said, "And when I see the blood, I will pass over you; and the plague shall not be on you to destroy you . . ." The blood was for the people's forgiveness. The blood covered the people's sins and appeased the righteous requirements of God.

Prayer . . .

Dear Lord, we intercede for brothers and sisters for this plague to pass over. You call us to pray for our leaders so we bring before You all those who are running the UK. We especially pray for our prime minister, Boris Johnson, who is in intensive care. We pray that he will get through this and come out stronger! We also lift up our neighbours, friends and family who are in intensive care. Lord, bring healing to the world! In Jesus' name. Amen!

8th April 2020

Pray for missionaries to rise up!

In the reign of Queen Victoria, from the mid-1850s to 1900, the British Empire was at its peak and Britain ruled the world. British missionaries were sent forth to the ends of the earth. From 1904 to 1950, great revivalists and evangelists emerged like Evan Roberts, George and Stephen Jeffreys, Smith Wigglesworth and the like. Then Great Britain turned their back on God, side-lining the Book of Books. Now, in this season when many of us are thinking about our own mortality, we prayer that revival will birth in people, to move them towards Christ. That during this time of difficulty, God will trigger inspiring missionaries and revivalists to shake up our country once again!

Prayer . . .

Dear Lord, it has been sometime since we have seen a massive move of the Holy Spirit in this country. So, we ask for You to bring a "tsunami" of Your mighty power. Let Covid-19 be removed, and Your name be brought in its place. Amen!

15

9th April 2020

Under normal circumstances during this Holy Week, there would be thousands of people gathering in churches to celebrate the resurrection of Christ. However, due to the seriousness of the virus pandemic the "lockdown" has meant we are unable to meet physically at church.

Jesus taught us to pray: "Thy kingdom come, Thy will be done in earth, as it is in heaven" (Matthew 6:10 KJV).

These words were part of a prayer by Jesus in what we know to be The Lord's Prayer, or we could say the disciples' prayer.

To enforce God's kingdom on earth takes praying up to the heavenlies. This prayer is God's rulership. It is God's rule for the lives of every person, families, professions, churches, workplaces, neighbourhoods, communities, cities, the NHS, marriages, governance, every circumstance, we want to see His kingdom established. The Bible tells us the kingdom is in us. So, we carry this with us. Jesus has given us the "keys" to His kingdom. We all hold this in our hands, to access and establish kingdom citizenship for those who don't know Him.

The Great Commission

"Then the eleven disciples went to Galilee, to the mountain where Jesus had told them to go. When they saw him, they worshipped him; but some doubted. Then Jesus came to them and said, 'All authority in heaven and on earth has been given

to me. Therefore go and make disciples of all nations, baptising them in the name of the Father and of the Son and of the Holy Spirit, and teaching them to obey everything I have commanded you. And surely I am with you always, to the very end of the age.'" (Matthew 28:16-20 NIV)

Prayer . . .

Dear Lord, we thank You that we carry something very precious in us, "Your kingdom", and wherever we go we can birth this throughout the world. We pray we will establish the Great Commission and see many come to Christ. Amen!

11th April 2020

Easter blessings

Between a rock and a hard place! Sometimes God uses events to bring out miracles we can so easily miss, and looking at the burial of Jesus Christ, we are face to face with some astonishing truth. I mean, generally all of us who are a part of the Christian faith are aware of the significance of the cross of Christ. But between the crucifixion and the resurrection there is the burial of Jesus. And at first thought it would seem to be anything but miraculous, a rather mundane and necessary act with little or no consequence except for what happens on both ends of it.

The burial of Jesus Christ is as supernatural and as miraculous in many ways as was His death and His resurrection. It is a marvellous and thrilling account of supernatural intervention in every detail in the life of Christ . . . from His birth to His burial to His resurrection, everything is controlled by God the Father for the fulfilment of divine purpose and prophecy.

Prayer . . .

Dear Father, there may be things in front of us now that seem mundane and insignificant, but they are there for a purpose, to fulfil Your entire will. Forgive us when we don't always look at the bigger picture and remember that everything is significant to You. Amen.

13th April 2020

Prevail and persist

During the week, I am able to pop into church to collect post, streamline messages, pray, but then I look at the empty chairs, at the stage where the worship team would normally be rehearsing, the children would be running around waving flags on Sunday morning, the prayer team seeking God; it saddens me and I'm longing for things to get back to normal. Then, the Lord led me to a story about Jacob in Genesis 32:22-29. A man wrestled with him until the breaking of the day. When the man saw that He did not prevail against Jacob, He touched his hip socket, and Jacob's hip was put out of joint as He wrestled with him. Then He said, "Let me go, for the day has broken." But Jacob said, "I will not let you go unless you bless me." And He said to him, "What is your name?" and he said, "Jacob." Then He said, "Your name shall no longer be called Jacob, but Israel, for you have struggled with God and with men, and have prevailed" (NKJV).

Prayer . . .

Dear Lord, help us to be persistent and be consistent in everything we do, even when things seem to be abnormal and unbalanced. Help us to stand firm so we can prevail, and when this season is over people will be running back to church and special blessing will prevail. Amen!

14th April 2020

Prophesy

I got up this morning at 5.38am, as the Lord quickened my spirit to read Acts 2:17.

> *"In the last days, God says, I will pour out my Spirit on all people. Your sons and daughters will prophesy, your young men will see visions, your old men will dream dreams."* (NIV)

Between Passover and Pentecost (Sunday 31st May 2020), there is to be a downturn of all pestilence and diseases. A word came to me: "He is calling His people to get ready, get into the upper room and start praying the Lord's Prayer over and over again," the prayer Jesus taught His disciples (Luke 11:2-4). "There will be a 'Great Awaking' around this planet, a tsunami is about to beseech us. This will be a 'milestone' in history and many who left their 'faith' will return. The truth (Jesus) will be known to those who don't believe, the trumpet will sound louder than before. My name (Jesus) will be called once again and there will be a 'purification', a cleansing and then a 'building' up of My churches throughout this land. Don't just be concerned about the future, but the 'now' and the 'present'; this is a time to 'stay' in the upper-room, where you can seek My face, humble yourself, so I can heal this land."

Prayer . . .

Dear Lord, during this season quicken our hearts and minds to seek Your face and hear from You so that we learn to draw from Your reservoir and lead towards greater times. Amen.

15th April 2020

Worship Him

Let's worship Him today at 3.00pm and give Him the glory! The worshippers the Father desires are those who worship "in spirit and in truth".

Rather He wants the human spirits of the worshippers to be engaged with His Spirit, allowing the worshipper to be drawn into unity with Him that He desires.

"God is spirit, and his worshippers must worship in the Spirit and in truth" (John 4:24 NIV). This is not an option, but a necessity. This is the way Christians must worship.

Prayer . . .

Dear Father, we pray that we will worship You today with all our body, soul and spirit. With some of us who have the time during this season and those on the frontline will just sing unto the Lord and give Him praise. Praise that will divert any sickness away from our bodies. In Jesus' name. Amen.

16th April 2020

Listening to God's prophetic Word

Praying for revelation and revival.

> *"To every thing there is a season, and a time to every purpose under the heaven. A time to be born . . ."* (Ecclesiastes 3:1, 2 KJV)

Story of encouragement

At the climax of the Azusa Street revival led by William Seymour, the city streets of Los Angeles had constant traffic jams and the city officials demanded the meeting be closed. The revival began in April 1906 and lasted 7 years. As it was winding up in May 1913, Seymour gave a prophecy that about 100 years from then, there would be a heaven-sent revival far greater than Azusa that would usher in the rapture. On that very same day, Charles Parham on the opposite side of America gave the same prophecy. He declared, "In 100 years, there will be another revival like Azusa and the Shekinah Glory will return. The coming move of God will be greater and farther reaching than Azusa. It will not be in one place only, or with a few, but all over the world. And it will not end but will culminate in the second coming of Christ."

The renowned evangelist Maria Woodworth Etter began a meeting on July 2nd, 1913 at Stone Church, Chicago, Illinois. The meeting was to be a 3-week camp meeting but revival broke out. The meeting went on for 6 months. Mass conversions, healings, deliverance and outpourings of the Spirit were common. Without advertisement, thousands came by every available means. From thousands of miles away and from near. At the climax of that meeting she stood and prophesied, "In 100 years there will be an outpouring of God's Spirit and His Shekinah Glory will be greater and more far reaching than that which was experienced at Azusa."

On the basis of these three prophecies, it behoves the church of today to rise up everywhere and pray down this revival.

> *"By the mouth of two or three witnesses every word shall be established."* (2 Corinthians 13:1; Matthew 18:16 NKJV)

Prayer . . .

Dear Lord, we pray that Your heart for this country will bring a new sense for change and revival. Whatever form it comes in, help us to be prepared for this new move of God. Amen!

17th April 2020

To fight for your body, soul and spirit

The charge to Timothy renewed:

> *"This charge I commit to you, son Timothy, according to the prophecies previously made concerning you, that by them you may wage the good warfare, having faith and a good conscience, which some having rejected, concerning the faith have suffered shipwreck, of whom are Hymenaeus and Alexander, whom I delivered to Satan that they may learn not to blaspheme."* (1 Timothy 1:18-20 NKJV)

Now, the key phrase that we noted at the end of verse 18, "fight a good warfare" or "fight a noble warfare" – I have taught this in my series on "Spiritual Warfare" to fight always in a noble manner, meaning be strategic for what is to come.

Prayer . . .

Dear Lord, we pray You will help those who are battling against the body, soul and spirit. We pray to push the enemy back, so we can move forward. Amen!

21st April 2020

"I don't just believe in prayer, I believe in answered prayer" – Pastor Jim Master.

When we research the scriptures and do a study of answered prayers, it becomes easy to believe how magnificent and glorious Jesus is.

The Bible teaches us of the power of prayer. I really believe that. I believe that prayer makes a difference; I believe that prayer is effective; I believe that prayer works. Abraham's servant prayed, and Rebekah appeared; Jacob wrestled and prayed, and prevailed with Christ; and Esau's mind was turned from twenty years of revenge. Joshua prayed, and Akan was discovered. Hannah prayed, and Samuel was born. David prayed, and Ahithophel hanged himself. Asa prayed, and victory was won. Jehoshaphat prayed, and God turned away his enemies. Isaiah and Hezekiah prayed, and in twelve hours a hundred and eighty five thousand Assyrians were slain. Mordecai and Esther prayed, and the plot to destroy the Jews was thwarted, and Haman was hanged on his own gallows. Ezra prayed at Ahava, and God answered.

Prayer . . .

Dear Lord, forgive us if we don't spend enough time praying and believing You are the answer to our prayers. Sometime the answer is "no" and other times "yes" . . . but you always answer! May we glorify You always! Amen.

22nd April 2020

Healing

When you receive a phone call and it's bad news – like yesterday we were told that our grandson Isaac stopped breathing and was rushed to hospital – there is a helplessness that rises up in you and you realise in that moment, the only thing you can do is pray. I travelled up to a hospital, which I could not enter due to Covid-19, and prayed outside, hoping God's power would heal my grandson, while also remembering all the other sick patients.

> *"And when the Lord saw her, he had compassion on her and said to her, 'Do not weep.' Then he came up and touched the bier, and the bearers stood still. And he said, 'Young man, I say to you, arise.' And the dead man sat up and began to speak, and Jesus gave him to his mother. Fear seized them all, and they glorified God, saying, 'A great prophet has arisen among us!' and 'God has visited his people!' And this report about him spread through the whole of Judea and all the surrounding country."* (Luke 7:13-17 ESV)

Prayer . . .

Dear Lord, we cannot be more amazed, over and over again, of the healing power of Your hand which is the gift You have given each one of us. May we be confident to use that gift to see many healed in the name of Jesus. Amen!

23rd April 2020

Covid-19 so surreal

For many of us, this season has been so surreal. It's like being in a movie and we are all acting. Sadly, we all know it is very real! We hear every day of families losing loved ones to this virus. The doctors, nurses, carers, cleaners, porters, etc., are working flat out and the government is providing a high level of benefits to a variety of people, businesses, employers, employees and many others. Yet, I read an interesting survey that many people want a new "normal" when this is over and appreciate life and nature more than they realised. A recent poll showed that only 9 per cent of people in Great Britain want to remove lockdown sooner rather than prolong it.

Even though we are to keep "social distancing", people are speaking to each other more than ever before and helping friends and neighbours with shopping, etc. More people are asking about the subject of "mortality" and life after death. It is a time for believers to rise up to the challenge and start to speak to our fellow neighbours about the Lord. To overcome fear with faith and breakthrough that "barrier of selfishness" and spread the Good News!

> *"How, then, can they call on the one they have not believed in? And how can they believe in the one of whom they have not heard? And how can they hear without someone preaching to them?"* (Romans 10:14 NIV)

Prayer . . .

Dear Lord, this season that appears to be unpredictable, is predicable by You and we pray that through the scriptures, we will have insight into greater things to come. Help us to place our security and dependency in You, Lord. Give us strength. Amen!

25th April 2020

It was vividly illustrated some years ago in Argentina. A missionary by the name of Miller went to Argentina with all sorts of plans for carrying out God's work. But God shut him up in a little mud church for more than a month and all he had to do was pray. He prayed until the spiritual powers controlling Argentina were brought into subjection. In that very strongly Roman Catholic country God miraculously opened the way for the largest stadium in the whole country to be taken over by a little insignificant American preacher whom nobody knew. At the end of a month, 200,000 people were gathering daily to listen to his message. This is one of the most remarkable moves of God recorded in church history and was the result of binding the unseen forces.

Prayer...

Dear Lord, we try to resolve many issues in our own strength. However, sometimes we are forced to isolate in order to seek Your face. In future, allow us to be more proactive in seeking Your presence. Amen.

27th April 2020

Who will stand in the gap?

God said in Ezekiel 22:30–31:

"I sought for a man among them who would make a wall, and stand in the gap before Me on behalf of the land, that I should not destroy it; but I found no one. Therefore have I poured out My indignation on them; I have consumed them with the fire of My wrath." (NKJV)

"If I could have found one man in all the nation," God said, "I could have spared them." Think of it! One man could have turned the tide for a whole nation. Yet there was not even one person willing to do it. This week is the time to stand in the "gap" and be that person.

We can turn families, friends, illnesses, disease and nations around by standing in the gap for our people. We have the authority and power in our hands!

Prayer . . .

Dear Lord, you said all authority has been given to us to trample on snakes and scorpions. Let us be the gap fillers that reach our hands out to those who need help and godly guidance. Use us! Amen.

28th April 2020

"They triumphed over him by the blood of the Lamb and by the word of their testimony; they did not love their lives so much as to shrink from death." (Revelation 12:11 NIV)

I had the chance to go shopping yesterday and had to queue up to get in the door. There were around 50 people ahead of me. I felt like going home, but was prompted by the Spirit to queue up like everyone else. When I joined in, I found the most amazing thing happened: people were chatting and having long conversations with each other and the friendliness – something I have not seen in years! The people at the checkout, the security guard and shoppers were so caring and considerate. It was a joy to see all this in the middle of the crisis.

I had a chance to witness to a few folk about what I do for a living, as pastor of a church, which was received very well. My thoughts are on people's perspective changing about God and life, and will more people seek Jesus during this time of crisis.

Prayer . . .

Dear Lord, I pray that every believer showing acts of kindness will show Jesus; we have a great opportunity to share more about our faith to others. For every believer there is a seeking soul out there waiting for us to speak to them. Give us courage! Amen.

29th April 2020

Why we need to pray for the government

In 1 Timothy 2:1-4:

Firstly: "Exhort first of all that supplications, prayers, intercessions, and giving of thanks be made for all men."

Secondly: "For kings and all who are in authority, that we may lead a quiet and peaceable life in all godliness and reverence."

Thirdly: "For this is good and acceptable in the sight of God our Saviour."

Fourthly: "Who desires all men to be saved and to come to the knowledge of the truth."

Prayer . . .

Dear Lord, we thank You for our government and ask for forgiveness when we have been critical instead of praying. Help us to be more grateful for what we have been provided with. Amen.

30th April 2020

How we can learn from this wilderness experience

During this season, which has been a "wilderness time", still there are lessons we can learn.

Firstly, it takes a humble attitude to learn from earthly tests. God not only wants us to endure tests, He wants us to learn from them. But we don't learn without humility. The proud don't learn.

In facts, Proverb 28:26 says

> *Whoever trusts in his own mind is a fool, but he who walks in wisdom will be delivered.* ESV.

And so the fool stews in the juices of his own ignorance. Some of you can read about these events, get up, and resume your life of grumbling as though you had never heard God speak. It can happen in any believer's life, anywhere in the world, going through any test. Biblical truth works, but it must be applied, regardless of your circumstances. Humility accelerates the learning process. Have you said to yourself lately, "Why don't we get through this situation and get on to something else?" Do you know why we don't? Because we refuse to learn from the same wilderness experience. Somehow, we just won't let it penetrate our hearts. But God never wastes His time or His tests on His people. He knows how long to plan the test, how often to repeat it, and how difficult the examination must be.

"When you pass through the waters, I will be with you; and when you pass through the rivers, they will not sweep over you. When you walk through the fire, you will not be burned; the flames will not set you ablaze." (Isaiah 43:2 NIV)

Prayer . . .

Dear Lord, this testing time has been difficult for all of us. Still, whatever You can teach us from this experience, please help us to learn. We pray that You will show us the way through every lesson, so we can progress to the next level in You. Amen.

30th April 2020

Honouring God through our giving

We are to honour God. That's what living as a faithful kingdom steward does – it honours God. We cannot give God anything that He doesn't already own. Which is why our thanksgiving and our vows (the things we pledge to do on behalf of His glory and advancing His kingdom) mean so much to Him. How we steward what has been given to us makes all the difference in the world. When we do that well, He says we can call upon Him and He will rescue us.

Prayer . . .

Dear Lord, we thank You that everything we have is Yours and the little we give back every week can be put to use to advance Your kingdom. We pray this will multiply and be used to win many for Christ. Let us not stop adding to the church and giving our first fruit. Amen.

3rd May 2020

How praising God can help us through depression!

I've always loved to listen to and play music. Music has a way of communicating the whole spectrum of human emotions, including fear, love, worship and sorrow.

As Martin Luther put it, "Music is the art of the prophets, the only art that can calm the agitations of the soul; it is one of the most magnificent and delightful presents God has given us."

And probably the greatest music book ever written is the book of Psalms. The Psalms were part of the public adoration of the Lord in ancient Israel. Though we don't know what the original melodies were, God made sure we have the lyrics.

In two psalms possibly influenced by David himself, Psalm 42 and 43, the sons of Korah wrote a worship song and gave it a slant – tackling the theme of brokenness and depression. Depression? you ask. How can that subject be in a worship song? Aren't all worship songs happy and uplifting? Not always!

> *"As the deer pants for streams of water, so my soul pants for you, my God. My soul thirsts for God, for the living God. When can I go and meet with God? My tears have been my food day and night, while people say to me all day long, 'Where is your God?'"* (Psalm 42:1-3 NIV)

Prayer . . .

Dear Lord, for those who are in lockdown and feeling sorrowful, we pray that their voices will be raised to the Lord and the grace of light will shine over the darkness. Amen.

5th May 2020

Last night I watched a film about Mother Teresa – a woman who gave her life to feed and nurse the poor, young and old, in Calcutta, India. She said that she was "the pencil in God's hand". She had a network of people around the world who would be prayer partners and would call them often and say "we need a 'storm prayer', please pray". When I think about those who give up their entire life for others with "unconditional love", as true sacrificial living. There are so many people around the world who have so little and complain about so little, and do it with a smile on their face! Whereas, there are also people who have everything and still complain about everything.

> *"Whoever is generous to the poor lends to the Lord, and he will repay him for his deed."* (Proverbs 19:17 ESV)

Prayer . . .

Dear Lord, we pray that more of us in the coming season will think about how we can provide for others unconditionally. Help us to step into this new season with clarity on the things we can do that will honour You. Amen.

7th May 2020

Dreams

A few weeks ago I had a peculiar dream. I was in a car park, in my car, but it had been stripped right down to the bear shell! No engine, tyres, seats, steering wheel, etc. This morning I got the interpretation of that dream. The Lord has brought us to a time of "stand still" and stripped away our regularity, so we can simply think and spend more time with Him. He made me think of things I wouldn't normally think about and speak to people I normally wouldn't speak to.

Throughout this time many of us will be thinking about church, fellowship, worship, prayer, all those things perhaps we have taken for granted and now miss very much. When we come back, let's return to a "new normal", after having reviewed our lives and time with God.

> *"He says, 'Be still, and know that I am God; I will be exalted among the nations, I will be exalted in the earth.'"* (Psalm 46:10 NIV)

Prayer . . .

Dear Lord, we have been in isolation and have had things stripped away in the last few weeks, which is especially hard as we have not been able to go to church. Forgive us that we have taken so many things for granted and teach us to spend this time preparing to do greater things in the future. Amen.

11th May 2020

One of my favourite psalms, which I read a lot when I was a child, is Psalm 42. This now reminds me of all those who have lost loved ones from the coronavirus and my heart goes out to every single one of the families.

> *"As the deer pants for the water brooks, so pants my soul for You, O God. My soul thirsts for God, for the living God. When shall I come and appear before God? My tears have been my food day and night, while they continually say to me, 'Where is your God?'"* (Psalm 42:1-3 NIV)

How many will be panting for answers to the burning question, "why"?

Prayer . . .

Dear Lord, we pray for everyone who has lost a loved one. So many will be asking questions and wanting answers to ease their pain. We pray they will find comfort and peace. Amen.

12th May 2020

Learning from our children!

"And they brought young children to him, that he should touch them: and his disciples rebuked those that brought them. But when Jesus saw it, he was much displeased, and said unto them, Suffer the little children to come unto me, and forbid them not: for of such is the kingdom of God. Verily I say unto you, Whosoever shall not receive the kingdom of God as a little child, he shall not enter therein. And he took them up in his arms, put his hands upon them, and blessed them."
(Mark 10:13-16 KJV)

The word says whoever shall receive the kingdom of God like a small child shall be the one to enter into God's kingdom. Adults can surely learn a lot from the character of little children. Children trust easily, especially their parents. They will jump off a counter into the arms of their parents trusting all the way that their parents will catch them and take care of them. Doubt doesn't enter their minds; they just dash forth. Out of the mouths of babes questions come forth that others may be afraid to ask. Little children just want to know the reason why. They don't use big words or pretence, just simply keep it real. They may not want to share their toys and will sometimes fight, but they also forgive and forget quickly and are friends again in an instant.

Prayer . . .

Dear Lord, we pray we become like children, brave, forgiving, loving and instinctive, to step out in faith. During this time we may need to step out without any fear, especially through this time of transition. This season could be very challenging for us as we prepare to move back into a "new normal". Lord, give us courage. Amen.

13th May 2020

The Lord forgives no matter what!

A Christian missionary recently met a fighter for ISIS (Islamic State of Iraq and Syria) who reported that he had dreamed of Jesus. He claimed to have killed many Christians and that he had enjoyed doing so, but that he had begun to have dreams of "a man in white" who appeared to him and told him, "You are killing My people." His certainty and belief in what he had been doing as a member of ISIS started to waver. Shortly afterward, just as he was about to execute one Christian, his victim told him, "I know you will kill me, but I give to you my Bible." He killed the man, but he took the Bible and began to read it. Jesus appeared to him in another dream and asked him to follow Him – an invitation the militant accepted. He reported this story to the missionary and asked to be discipled.

Prayer . . .

Dear Lord, we thank You that no one is exempt from the kingdom of heaven, for whoever calls on His name will be saved! Amen.

14th May 2020

The journey of being locked up

A prominent Christian counsellor once said something that happened to him when he was three years old which made him think, that is what the Christian life is going to be like for me. He recalled: "I decided I was a big boy and could use the bathroom without anyone's help. So I climbed the stairs, closed and locked the door behind me, and for the next few minutes felt very self-sufficient." After he was done, though, he couldn't unlock the door. He banged on the door, got everyone's attention, and started a small panic. His father thought quickly, got out a ladder, ran it up the side of the house, prised open the window, climbed into the room, went past his son, and with one movement jerked open the door, unlocking it and freeing his son – who promptly ran out to play!

The counsellor reflected that, even as a grown-up, he thought that every time he had a difficulty, God would show up, unlock the door, and spring him free. However, sometimes the journey about being locked up teaches us much more than the destination we wish to arrive at.

Prayer . . .

Dear Lord, we pray that You will give us all patience during this time and help us to learn from every aspect of this journey and see how we can help others. Many thanks. Amen.

18th May 2020

Each of my two grandsons have their own distinct personality; even as babies, just a few days old, they had their own way of expressing their needs.

They both reached their first birthday this month and have grown quickly! They are developing their likes and dislikes, and observing their strengths and weaknesses has been interesting and lots of fun! When you see your grandchildren excelling in a specific area, it is encouraging. So, I will always ask the Lord to stir up their gifts and use them for His glory.

In the same way, when I see people who have developed gifts and talents, it may very well be a part of the calling that God has placed on their life. The gift they are enjoying now may even give them some insight to the things that God has purposed for the future. A finger painter today may be a Van Gogh tomorrow!

> *"Whatever you do, work at it with all your heart, as working for the Lord, not for human Master, since you know that you will receive an inheritance from the Lord as a reward. It is the Lord Christ you are serving."* (Colossians 3:23-24 NIV)

Prayer . . .

Dear Lord, we pray that every believer uses their talent and gifting to glorify God and nothing is used to glorify ourselves. We pray one day everyone will be applauding You for Your precious gift of Your Son, You sent to die on the cross. Amen.

19th May 2020

Overcoming depression

One reason for spiritual depression is unfulfilled expectations. We all have expectations and when they go unmet, especially when it comes to a trial in life as a Christian, the result may be spiritual depression.

In Psalm 42, the psalmist described his thirst for God's presence and comfort, as well as his inability to have them: "When I remember these things, I pour out my soul within me. For I used to go with the multitude; I went with them to the house of God, with the voice of joy and praise, with a multitude that kept the pilgrim feast" (v. 4 NKJV). He felt cut off from spiritual life, unable to enjoy expected refreshment and relief. Like a thirsty deer, winded and desperate for water, he found no reprieve.

> *Solomon declared, "Hope deferred makes the heart sick, but a longing fulfilled is a tree of life"* (Proverbs 13:12 NIV).

During this difficult season, when the world has been hit by the pandemic, many people are thirsting for the church doors to be open and are longing to fellowship again.

Prayer . . .

Dear Lord, we pray for those people who are depressed during this time. We pray they feel nourished and fed by our prayers and Your Word. We pray that the church's doors will be opening soon so God's people can worship You together again. Amen.

20th May 2020

Choices we need to make in the next few weeks

A man visited his family doctor concerned that he was losing his memory. After an examination, the doctor said, "I really can't help fix the memory problem without impairing your eyesight. You have a difficult choice: Do you want to remember or do you want to see?" The man thought for a moment and replied, "I'll take my eyesight over my memory, for I would rather see where I am going than remember where I have been." What would you choose? We all stand on the brink of an unknown future in Covid-19. Often we gaze into tomorrow's mist, trying to make out distant landmarks. Frustrated, we glance at the past, hoping things in our lives will improve.

> *"The mind of man plans his way, but the Lord directs his steps."* (Proverbs 16:9 NASB)

Prayer . . .

Dear Lord, we pray for the decisions we need to make in the next few weeks. This may be very difficult for some people who have to make new choices. For some, it will be entering church for the very first time. May we welcome them in this hard time and help guide them to make the right choice. We pray God will draw people to Christ. Amen.

26th May 2020

Behind both the 1740 American Great Awakening and the British 1740–1790 Methodist Revival lies the prayer life and nurturing role of Susanna Wesley. She was married to a preacher, Samuel Wesley. They had 19 children, nine of whom died in infancy. Out of the 10 who survived, one was disabled and another was mute for many years. Her husband, although a minister, was not committed to his family. He left her to raise her children alone for a long period of time. Debts plagued their home, which was often left with no food and no money. At one point he was imprisoned due to financial indebtedness. Twice their home was burned to the ground. They lost everything they ever had twice over. It was in one of those fires that John Wesley was rescued as a small child, like "a brand plucked from the fire" (Zechariah 3:2). Yet in the midst of all this, she nurtured two children of revival, Charles and John Wesley. She personally home-schooled all her children. She taught them Theology, English, Mathematics, French and other subjects. She made a covenant with God to give Him two hours every day. How God can birth revival in anyone who spends time with Him!

> "And we know that for those who love God all things work together for good, for those who are called according to his purpose." (Romans 8:28 ESV)

Prayer . . .

Dear Lord, sometimes we don't realise the time we spend with You births revival and changes things around us. Amen!

27th May 2020

Reading about Job today, I can't help thinking about those families who have lost their lives.

Job was a man of unparalleled and genuine piety. He was also a man of well-deserved prosperity. He was a godly gentleman, extremely wealthy, a fine husband, and a faithful father. In a quick and brutal sweep of back-to-back calamities, Job was reduced to a twisted mass of brokenness and grief. The extraordinary accumulation of disasters that hit him would have been enough to finish off any one of us living today. Job is left bankrupt, homeless, helpless, and childless. He's left standing beside the ten fresh graves of his now-dead children on a windswept hill. His wife is heaving deep sobs of grief as she kneels beside him, having just heard him say, "Whether our God gives to us or takes everything from us, we will follow Him." She leans over and secretly whispers, "Just curse God and die."

"The Lord gave and the Lord has taken away; may the name of the Lord be praised." (Job 1:21 NIV)

Prayer . . .

Dear Lord, how could anyone comprehend that a few months ago, this country would witness over 36,000 people lost to a virus and the country would be in "lockdown". The world has been turned upside down in such a short time. As Christians we put our trust in God and continue to remember to pray for those who have lost loved ones and pray they will reach out to Jesus. Amen.

28th May 2020

Prayer for protection!

"His sons used to go and hold a feast in the house of each one on his day, and they would send and invite their three sisters to eat and drink with them. When the days of feasting had completed their cycle, Job would send and consecrate them, rising up early in the morning and offering burnt offerings according to the number of them all; for Job said, 'Perhaps my sons have sinned and cursed God in their hearts.' Thus Job did continually." (Job 1:4-5 NASB)

By offering up ten burnt offerings in the name of each young adult, he was concerned that in their hearts there may have been a hint of disobedience or perhaps one of them told an off-coloured story during their frequent get-togethers. Job is diligent deep within – spiritually sensitive not only regarding his life, but for the walk and talk of his children. Praying man. Pure man. Priestly man. Faithful man. What a man!

Prayer . . .

Dear Lord, we pray every day for those we love. We pray for protection over those who are very close to us. We anticipate great things for our friends and family to come to Christ and offer up our prayers for each one. Amen!

1st June 2020

Anniversary!

I would never have imagined that we would be celebrating our 35th wedding anniversary in a season of "lockdown"! But, no matter what the circumstances, nothing can take away from that one special day when we made a covenant before God and placed wedding rings to seal the deal. In the same way, those who accept Christ have made a covenant with Him and He has sealed a promise of redemption, inheritance and eternal life. One day there will be a very special marriage, this will be the "marriage supper of the lamb" and Christians will be taken up into heaven celebrating Christ's victory over this earth!

"'Let us rejoice and be glad and give him glory! For the wedding of the Lamb has come, and his bride has made herself ready. Fine linen, bright and clean, was given her to wear.' (Fine linen stands for the righteous acts of God's holy people.) Then the angel said to me, 'Write this: Blessed are those who are invited to the wedding supper of the Lamb!' And he added, 'These are the true words of God.' At this I fell at his feet to worship him. But he said to me, 'Don't do that! I am a fellow servant with you and with your brothers and sisters who hold to the testimony of Jesus. Worship God! For it is the Spirit of prophecy who bears testimony to Jesus.'" (Revelation 19:7-10 NIV)

Prayer . . .

Thank you, Lord, that even though the marriage on this earth may be temporary, the covenant with You is eternal. As believers we can be assured that we have a new life to look forward to and a celebration is waiting for us. Amen!

2nd June 2020

Faith and hope

Two of the key things to the gospel of Christ are "faith and hope". If we don't believe in these, then we are like sheep gone astray!

We are hearing more and more on the news about the easing of lockdown and how slowly we are taking steps closer to meeting our fellow brothers and sisters. For some, they have only just begun to appreciate freedom after several weeks in isolation. As Christians, we know that real freedom and peace can only be found in knowing Christ and believing that He ascended into heaven and left us His Holy Spirit to take His place to live in each one to guide and comfort us.

> *"Therefore encourage one another and build one another up, just as in fact you are doing."* (1 Thessalonians 5:11 NIV)

> *"Not neglecting to meet together, as is the habit of some, but encouraging one another, and all the more as you see the Day drawing near."* (Hebrews 10:25 ESV)

Prayer . . .

Dear Lord, we have taken things for granted and made assumptions, the state of the nation has been turned upside down in the last three months and our freedom has been taken away. We pray we never take things for granted and learn to appreciate all that we have been given by You. We thank You for our church and fellow brothers and sisters. Our faith and hope is in You. Amen.

3rd June 2020

God will build His Church

I will be entering the church today to plan for re-opening in July. Seeing the building God has given us and reflecting on the years we have spent decorating, refurbishing, planning ministry, all of this so His name may be glorified. This church has seen many new faces walking through the doors and people coming to Christ, missions set up in India and Africa, events such as International food night, Bible school, children's work, youth work, men's, women's and seniors, etc.; then suddenly all this is put on hold for a small period of time – still you can praise God and wonder at His gift of how precious life is.

Jesus said, "I will build my church." Not destroy it. It's so important to heaven, that the church manifests itself here on earth, so the gates of hell will not prevail.

> *"And I tell you that you are Peter, and on this rock I will build my church, and the gates of Hades will not overcome it."*
> (Matthew 16:18 NIV)

Prayer . . .

Dear Lord, when You provide us with people who help us to grow Your church and leaders who never compromise to do their best for the sake of the kingdom, we can only be thankful to You. We pray You will continue to build Your church around the world to be strong and formidable. Amen!

4th June 2020

Cleansing

As our church carpets were being cleaned and sanitised, I could see a big difference in the before and after and it reminded me of the story of Jesus when He went into the temple and turned the tables upside down saying, "'My house will be called a house of prayer,' but you are making it 'a den of robbers'" (Matthew 21:13 NIV).

Thankfully we have not made this a den of robbers! Cleaning and sanitising reminds me how powerful salvation is and how it cleanses a person's life to make them new. It may not be sanitation, but certainly sanctification, being set apart to fulfil God's service.

Prayer . . .

Dear Lord, we thank You that You chose to die and set us apart from the world's temptations and to live renewed lives, with new thinking and perspective. We pray we continue to look to You for our cleaning. Amen.

8th June 2020

"Fear not, for I am with you; be not dismayed, for I am your God. I will strengthen you, yes, I will help you, I will uphold you with My righteous right hand." (Isaiah 41:10 NKJV)

It is a great comfort to know that we are not to fear or be dismayed knowing God is with us and He is here to help. Sometimes, this can feel a little unbalanced especially when life throws things at us that are unexpected. When reading this small passage, Isaiah says that the Lord will uphold us with His righteousness. That is doing what is good. No matter what the circumstances we are to make the right choices for the Lord is righteous, and take no shortcuts and then He will "uphold" us every day. Our strength comes from doing the right thing.

Prayer . . .

Dear Lord, we know how hard it can be sometimes to make a decision through our own eyes, but we need to make these decisions through the Spirit. Please strengthen us each day to do the right thing. Amen.

9th June 2020

Ephesians 2:7 gives us a glimpse into the preeminent role grace plays, not only now but for all eternity. It says, "That in the ages to come He might show the exceeding riches of His grace in His kindness towards us in Christ Jesus" (NKJV). Grace is never-ending. There will be so much grace in heaven that it will blow your mind! In fact, God will even remove night and our desire for sleep so that we can stay awake all the time in order to fully bask in the glory of His grace (Revelation 22:5). That's how much this supernatural provision of grace in eternity will be.

Prayer . . .

Dear Lord, we continue to pray for Your grace so we can show this towards the people surrounding us. We know it's only by Your power released in us that we are able to use this gift of grace and build on our character. Amen.

50

10th June 2020

Last night I had a Zoom meeting with my leadership team and it made me think how God hasn't called us to be independent, but interdependent, to rely on each other. The creation in the book of Genesis shows us how everything has a purpose and is connected to each other. When we start to only depend on ourselves, this is when we come out of God's divine order. There are many people in this pandemic who have realised that they need "someone" after having suffered because of the consequences. Remember what Jesus said, "For where two or three are gathered together in my name, there am I in the midst of them" (Matthew 18:20 KJV).

Prayer . . .

Dear Lord, we thank You that people are realising they need to reach out and connect to somebody, and that You created us to be a part of a bigger family. We pray we continue to reach out to those who need help and support. Amen.

15th June 2020

"Come to Me, all you who labour and are heavy laden, and I will give you rest." (Matthew 11:28 NKJV*)*

It has been mentioned many times that what has happened in the last few months is "unprecedented". That is to say it is unknown, never done before or ever experienced. This is true for many in our lifetimes. We don't have answers to every question. The loss of a loved one, the illness of a friend, those feeling lonely and many feeling depressed. We are in a season that many of us will never be able to forget. It will go down in history and future generations will be reading about this, but one thing we can be certain of is the promise Christ gives to those who are heavy laden: there is rest in Him.

Prayer . . .

Dear Lord, we ask for those who have lost family members in this season, that they will find rest in You. We know life is so short, but we are eternally grateful that for Christians life begins after our time on earth. Amen!

18th June 2020

John Owen, the great Puritan commentator, wrote these words, "A minister may fill his pews, his communion roll, the mouths of the public, but what that minister is on his knees in secret before Almighty God, that he is and no more."

And what John Owen is saying is what the Scripture certainly sets forth: that the demand of God for one in ministry goes beyond ability, it goes even beyond giftedness; it goes all the way to character.

Prayer . . .

We thank You, Lord, that You don't look at our outward appearance, but at the heart. We thank You that You laid down the Fruit of the Spirit to be key in our lives: love, joy, peace, patience, kindness, goodness, faithfulness, gentleness, and self-control. Amen.

22nd June 2020

"I tell you, open your eyes and look at the fields! They are ripe for harvest." (John 4:35 NIV)

It takes four months for the wheat to be ready to harvest. But souls are out there now ready to be harvested for the kingdom of God. Jesus sowed a single seed into the heart of many men. One seed you sow into people can produce the next massive harvest for the kingdom of God! It is time for us to continue to sow seeds into the hearts of people and pray they may be prepared to listen to the gospel of Christ.

Prayer . . .

Dear Lord, we pray we don't take our focus away from the main purpose of sowing seeds of salvation into people's hearts. We pray that as the opportunity opens up to us, we won't let our hearts be hardened by recent events. Amen.

54

23rd June 2020

A recent article from Mervyn Thomas of CSW:

"The coronavirus pandemic has had a profound effect in all of the countries in which we work. In Pakistan, some Christian communities have been discriminated against and denied food aid, with reports of over 100 Christian families excluded from receiving assistance in one incident alone. In China, over one million Uyghur Muslims and those from other ethnic groups are confined in 're-education camps' because of their ethnicity and religion. Conditions there are dangerously unsanitary and overcrowded. This human rights crisis could now be compounded by this a deadly outbreak on a massive scale. In Mexico, Christian families have had their water and sewage services cut off because of their beliefs. They can't perform the basic hygiene of washing their hands, which would help protect them during the coronavirus outbreak. These groups were already at great risk, regularly facing discrimination, violence or worse because of their religious beliefs. Today they are at risk of being targeted even further."

Prayer . . .

Dear Lord, we hear how other countries are struggling around the world, unable to get the very basic hygiene equipment, and discriminated against because of their faith. We thank You, God, that many of us don't have to worry about these things as we have all we need. So, Lord, we pray aid will be sent to those in need as soon as possible and they receive all the help needed. Amen.

40 Days of Prayer and Fasting
Always seek medical advice before you begin.

FIRST WEEK

	DAY 1	DAY 2	DAY 3	DAY 4	DAY 5	DAY 6	DAY 7
ONE MEAL							
TWO MEALS							
ALL MEALS							

SECOND WEEK

	DAY 1	DAY 2	DAY 3	DAY 4	DAY 5	DAY 6	DAY 7
ONE MEAL							
TWO MEALS							
ALL MEALS							

THIRD WEEK (21 DAYS)

	DAY 1	DAY 2	DAY 3	DAY 4	DAY 5	DAY 6	DAY 7
ONE MEAL							
TWO MEALS							
ALL MEALS							

FOURTH WEEK

	DAY 1	DAY 2	DAY 3	DAY 4	DAY 5	DAY 6	DAY 7
ONE MEAL							
TWO MEALS							
ALL MEALS							

FIFTH WEEK

	DAY 1	DAY 2	DAY 3	DAY 4	DAY 5	DAY 6	DAY 7
ONE MEAL							
TWO MEALS							
ALL MEALS							

SIXTH WEEK (40 DAYS!)

	DAY 1	DAY 2	DAY 3	DAY 4	DAY 5
ONE MEAL					
TWO MEALS					
ALL MEALS					